SAVIOR
— OF THE —
NATIONS

DAILY DEVOTIONS

Library of Congress Cataloging-in-Publication Data

Day, J. Bart

Savior of the Nations : daily devotions / J. Bart Day.

p. cm.

ISBN 978-0-7586-1488-9

1. Advent—Meditations. 2. Christmas—Meditations. I. Title.

BV40.D39 2009

242'.33—dc22

2009004364

1 2 3 4 5 6 7 8 9 10   18 17 16 15 14 13 12 11 10 09

DAILY DEVOTIONS

SAVIOR
OF THE
NATIONS

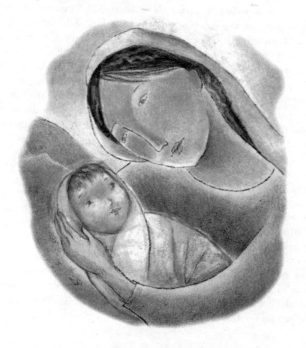

J. BART DAY

CONCORDIA PUBLISHING HOUSE · SAINT LOUIS

And the Word became flesh and dwelt among us,
and we have seen His glory, glory as of the only Son
from the Father, full of grace and truth. (John 1:14)

He Comes!

Advent is a time of preparation. Advent, in Latin, means, "he comes." In that sense, Advent is a confession of the faith that the Word who was there at the beginning, before the dawn of time, comes. Not "he came," but rather, "he comes." He continues to come to us as He is, the Word, not only through the hearing of the Scriptures and the preaching of Himself in all purity and truth, but He continues to come in His enfleshed self, through His body and blood in the Lord's Supper. He who was there before the dawn of time comes for us.

John the evangelist, while writing his Gospel, knew that there were already in his day (and probably assumed there would be in the future) those who would doubt who Jesus really was. There were some who would say the divinity of God could never suffer death on the cross. The purity of God would never pollute itself so radically as to become flesh. Jesus must have only just appeared to be human. Others would say that Jesus was someone special, but not really divine. Both ideas rob us of the joy of salvation in knowing that He was "tempted as we are, yet without sin" (Hebrews 4:15) and that "the Word became flesh and dwelt among us" (John 1:14).

The Advent season focuses our attention not only on what happened at a manger in Bethlehem but also on what happened on a cross at Golgotha, what continues to happen at the altar of the Lord, and what will happen on the Last Day. He comes.

He was in the world, and the world was made through Him,
yet the world did not know Him. (John 1:10)

Virgin's Son, Make Here Your Home!

Everywhere we go this time of year, the stores are filled with Christmas music and Christmas decorations. We seem to be cheerier and a little more aware of the needs of the less fortunate in the world. That there seems to be something special in the air is acknowledged even by those who are not particularly religious. In ancient times, pagans began festivals celebrating the lengthening of the day after the winter solstice. The celebration of Jesus' birth in December came to coincide with some of those festivals in various places in the Northern Hemisphere. Christians are sometimes embarrassed by those pagan festivals that our forefathers co-opted. But is this not something like the creation waiting "with eager longing for the revealing of the sons of God" (Romans 8:19) and the crying out of the very stones themselves (Luke 19:40)? Some insist that this longing for peace and goodwill toward others is an indicator that there is a God who will bring peace and reconciliation to the world.

Although the world longs for reconciliation, much of the world is still locked in its denial of the reconciliation Jesus came to bring. The good news is that Jesus entered into our world to save us and to restore to us our "right to become children of God" (John 1:12). In the first stanza of "Savior of the Nations, Come" there is a gentle imploring of the Lord to come and be in this world for us. Christians can join with all creation in praise that Jesus left heaven and has brought reconciliation to the world. There is something in the air this time of year. It is the embodiment of the longing that the Lord would make good on His promise to return and set to right all of creation, all of heaven and earth. Come, Lord Jesus. Amen.

And the Word became flesh and dwelt among us.
(John 1:14a)

That the Lord Chose
Such a Birth

Body is an elegant word; we use it to describe the beautiful form of a sleek sports car or even the character of wine. But *flesh* is a word that just has a visceral quality to it. There is no way to pretty it up. This word would strike John's Greek-speaking listeners as even less sophisticated than it does to us. In Greek philosophy, nothing divine would ever be associated with anything fleshly. To say that the divine Word became flesh would be simply barbaric.

Athanasius, an early fourth-century Church Father famous for the creed named after him, wrote: "For the Word perceived that was the only way that the corruption of the people could be undone. However, it was impossible for the Word to suffer death, being immortal and Son of the Father. Therefore, He takes to Himself a body capable of death, so that such a body, by partaking of the Word who is above all, might be worthy to die in the place of all, and might because of the Word that had come to dwell in it, remain incorruptible."

We marvel that Jesus, our Savior, gave up the perfect joy of heaven in order to be born of a woman and to take on human flesh and all that entails: our hunger, our thirst, our weakness, our ultimate limitedness. "For our sake [God] made Him to be sin who knew no sin, so that in Him we might become the righteousness of God" (2 Corinthians 5:21). It is Jesus' great gift to us that He shares in the same flesh and blood we have and was subject to suffering and death as we are. Jesus destroyed death by dying to it. He rendered death powerless that death might lose its power and sting (Hebrews 2:14). Thanks be to God that He who created the flesh of Adam took on Adam's flesh for us and for our salvation.

And the Word became flesh and dwelt among us.
(John 1:14a)

Make Here Your Home!

Just before Jesus ascends to heaven, He says to the disciples, "I am with you always, to the end of the age" (Matthew 28:20). This passage has been particularly comforting to Christians throughout the ages, especially during times of hardship and persecution. And the message is sure and true. The bodily-resurrected Jesus is promising not just to be with us in His spirit but He is promising to be with us even as He bodily ascends to heaven.

Some believers have had a difficult time understanding this abiding presence of Jesus as being anything more than like when we tell our children we cannot be at their recital or ballgame, but we will be with them in spirit. To do this is to spiritualize Jesus—a very dangerous idea that would rob us of the comfort of the Lord's abiding presence if we let it. After He was resurrected, Jesus went through great pains to show that He was not merely a spirit. He showed the disciples the physical wounds in His hands and side (John 20:20). He told Thomas to put his hand in His side and touch His wound (John 20:27). He asked for something to eat in Galilee (Luke 24:43). The resurrected Jesus has His glorified physical body. He continues to be present with us both as true God and as true man.

On the contrary, Jesus is also the Word made flesh. He is the Word of God, and He is where His Word is. Just as Jesus became flesh and tabernacled here among us during His earthly life and ministry, so also He is at His altar where He puts into our mouths His body and blood. While we do not understand precisely how it is that the Lord can remain both at God's right hand in heaven and be with us by His body and blood, we will rejoice that He not only dwelt among us long ago but also is now really present with us forever. Amen.

*In Him was life, and the life was the light of men. The light
shines in the darkness, and the darkness has not overcome it.
(John 1:4–5)*

From the Manger
Newborn Light

Scientists have long known that all the energy on our planet comes
from our sun. The coal, oil, and gas deposits deep in our earth
were once plant and animal material storing the energy of the sun
from millennia ago in an ultradense and efficient form. While all the con-
troversy swirls surrounding carbon-based fuels, there is no doubt those
fuels have brought light and prolonged life to billions of people on our
planet for generations.

In the prologue to his Gospel, John makes a number of allusions back
to the creation account in Genesis 1. One that is quite profound is when
John calls Jesus "the light of men." When we read the creation account,
we see that everything was formless and empty; there was nothing but
darkness. And God spoke, "Let there be light," and by speaking it, by
the Word, it came to be (Genesis 1:3), and that light came and gave life
to what became a planet filled with every sort of living thing, plant and
animal, including Adam and Eve and their descendants.

In a manger in Bethlehem, some 2,000 years ago, once again, He
who always was, and by whom all flesh was made, took on flesh Himself.
The Light and Life was born into a world darkened by sin and death. The
Word once again entered the darkness, and by being there, destroyed the
darkness and brought life to the whole world and everything in it. By
coming into our world, Jesus meant to redeem it and restore to it the
life and light that all people need in order to really see and to really live.
Contrary to some Eastern philosophies, light and darkness are not equals.
Even the smallest flicker of light easily overcomes darkness. How much
greater then, has the darkness of sin and death been overcome than by the
birth of the light of the world who shines brighter than the sun!

In Him was life, and the life was the light of men.
(John 1:4)

Shines in Glory
Through the Night

When the Lord led Israel out of Egypt, He led them by personally dwelling with His people in a pillar of cloud by day and pillar of fire by night. The cloud protected Israel from Pharaoh's chariots as they walked across the seabed of the Red Sea. The pillar of fire lit up the night for miles so that all of Israel would know that even in the midst of the dangers of night the Lord their God was with them. He who rescued them from slavery in Egypt had not led them into the wilderness to be lost, but He dwelt with them in a real and physical way.

When Jesus was born into the world, He brought with Him all of His glory, and yet it was hidden. Jesus' birth, apart from the angelic pronouncements, was very ordinary—as ordinary as was almost every other day of Jesus' earthly life. For John the evangelist, Jesus' glory peeks through at the signs, the miracles Jesus does so that others may believe in Him. The wedding at Cana (2:11), the healings, feeding the five thousand, and even Jesus' teachings, reveal tiny glimpses of Jesus' glory. In these ways, the Light that shined in the darkness has again shined in the world darkened by sin.

John records the raising of Lazarus and makes plain that Jesus raises Lazarus to glorify the Lord and the one He sent (11:4, 40). For John, the crucifixion of Jesus is the revelation of God's glory, and we would not know it except by the High Priestly Prayer: "And now, Father, glorify Me in Your own presence with the glory that I had with You before the world existed" (17:5). This the Father did most clearly and most certainly for us at Jesus' cross. On that high pillar, God showed the purpose of His abiding presence in the world: to redeem it. Jesus' light still shines in the darkness, and the darkness cannot overcome it.

The light shines in the darkness,
and the darkness has not overcome it. (John 1:5)

Darkness There No More Resides

Driving through neighborhoods at night this time of year is usually a real treat. Many people hang lights on their houses and in their trees and bushes, turning the normal drive into a fantasyland of lights that chase away the darkness.

There seems to be a primal yearning to push back against encroaching darkness. John understands this fundamental longing of people. For him, light was a metaphor for the Gospel. Jesus declared Himself to be the light of the world not once but twice (8:12; 9:5), perhaps even three times if you count 12:46 where Jesus says that He came as light into the world so that all who believe in Him would not remain in darkness. John develops the contrast between light and darkness as the contrast between the Light and the Darkness—between Jesus and the world—to show very clearly what Jesus did by coming into the world to save all people from their sin. In Jesus' conversation with Nicodemus, He has an extended explanation that the light He brings into the world is judgment on sin and those who love the darkness (3:19–21), and this is the explanation for His being sent into the world by the Father (3:16).

The parallel verse to 1 John 1:8–9, which we know from the confession of sin in our liturgy, comes just before in verses 6–7: "If we say we have fellowship with Him while we walk in darkness, we lie and do not practice the truth. But if we walk in the light, as He is in the light, we have fellowship with one another, and the blood of Jesus His Son cleanses us from all sin." Jesus entered the world darkened by sin and brought light. Now darkness no more resides where the bright beams of Jesus' righteousness shines. Amen.

And the Word became flesh and dwelt among us,
and we have seen His glory, glory as of the only Son
from the Father, full of grace and truth. (John 1:14)

The Word of God Made Flesh

Often we see news coverage of government officials purposely taking time to meet and speak with the "regular folks"—especially if they are campaigning for election. Voters seem to like politicians who are just like them.

In the early centuries of the Church, during the controversies around the human and divine natures of Christ, one of the biggest stumbling blocks for people was that Jesus could not be "just like us" if He was going to be worthy of worship and adoration. For Greek Christians, who were used to the myths in which the gods took the forms of people, no god worth his salt would actually be enfleshed. It would taint his divine essence.

But the divine Word became flesh, says John. He through whom all the world was made did not consider it unworthy of Himself to put on flesh and dwell among us but did so that we might become God's children and His brothers and sisters. Jesus took on our flesh so that He could live under the Law and fulfill it in every way (Galatians 4:4–5), and so that He would be able to suffer and die in our place (Isaiah 53). Amen!

For to us a child is born, to us a son is given;
and the government shall be upon His shoulder,
and His name shall be called Wonderful Counselor, Mighty
God, Everlasting Father, Prince of Peace. (Isaiah 9:6)

The Word Was Made Flesh
and Dwelt Among Us

There are a number of Christians who probably cannot read the verse above without the great strains of Handel's *Messiah* bouncing along in their head. It is almost like those biblical canticles we sing in our liturgies—the words and the tunes have become integrated, a single thing.

When the eternal Word became flesh, He became completely and inseparably integrated with all of humanity for the remainder of eternity. Perhaps we have seen too many cartoons where the spirit of the character wearing angel wings separates from its dead body, but sometimes Christians have a difficult time with the idea that this fleshly body is not just something temporary for us. Nor was it for Jesus. Jesus was born as God's Son but also as Mary's. He is inseparably bound to the flesh He took when He entered this world. It was that flesh which was resurrected from the tomb and it was that flesh in which Thomas and the other disciples saw the spear and nail wounds. Jesus ascended to the right hand of the Father in both resurrected flesh and spirit. Jesus gives us that resurrected flesh when He gathers us around His altar and says, "Take; eat. This is My body, which is given for you" (Matthew 26:26; Luke 22:19). By His Word, He binds His body and blood to the bread and the wine.

When we eat and drink the body and blood of the Lord, He makes one more union—Himself to us. This is how we behold His glory. This is how He fills us with His grace and truth. We need not worry how He is doing it but merely trust in His word, the Word that is inseparably bound in and with the bread and wine and declares those elements to be His body and blood for us and for the forgiveness of sins. Amen.

For to us a child is born, to us a son is given.
(Isaiah 9:6)

The Word of God Made Flesh

Governments large and small employ ambassadors and envoys to travel to other countries, put a "good face" on their policies, and promote mutual understanding and cooperation between nations. Often the success or failure of foreign relations rests in how well diplomats get along personally rather than merely officially. Many times, diplomats sent to foreign countries are people who have lived, worked, or studied in the countries to which they are sent so that they have some connection and understanding of the people they will work with.

This is an interesting idea because that is exactly what God the Father did in sending His Son, Jesus, into the flesh, to be born of the Spirit as a child of a human mother. Jesus left the splendor of heaven and came to dwell among the people. He knew them. They had been created through Him. He had come many times simply as the Word of God, but this time He came as that Word of God embodied, or as John says, "the Word became flesh" (1:14). The Father sent His Son to take on the flesh of the very people He had brought into existence. By His taking on the flesh He would understand us perfectly, and we would fully understand the loving heart of God.

The very Son of God came to earth so that God's people would never doubt the heart and the intentions of God their heavenly Father. If ever we wanted to know God and know about God, we can know Him perfectly by the one whom He sent: Jesus Christ. Jesus dwelt among us knowing all our hurts and sorrows, pains and losses. He experienced our worries, and He bore our sins. He even experienced our death so that we might experience the new life He came to bring. Amen.

For to us a child is born, to us a son is given.
(Isaiah 9:6)

Woman's Offspring, Pure and Fresh

In Lutheran churches today, Mary, the mother of our Lord, perhaps does not get quite the attention she deserves. That probably has a great deal to do with some of the abuses of the Roman Catholic Church in ascribing to Mary qualities and attributes that the Scriptures never give her. But it is something of a loss for us that we feel the need to be hypersensitive about saying too much about Mary. If Gabriel can call her "O favored one" (Luke 1:28), and her cousin Elizabeth can call her "blessed" (Luke 1:42), perhaps we can too!

We have marveled that the Lord would choose such a birth, but the blessed Virgin Mary was the vessel whom God the Father chose to bear His Son into the world. But what was in her womb was not there by the result of normal human relations. The Spirit of God had rested upon her in a way unique in human history. In no other way could the eternal Word take on flesh in the most human way.

Greek and Roman myths are filled with stories of the gods taking human form and dwelling on earth with mortals. But this is not what happened with Jesus. Jesus did not take on a human body or take the shape of a man; He became flesh. He was conceived of the Holy Spirit, gestated in a human womb, and born of a human mother, taking on that flesh without taking on her sin and without inheriting the original sin passed through normal human conception. It is no small wonder, then, that we should call Mary blessed, because the fruit of her womb was indeed blessed, and through Him the entire world has been blessed. Thanks be to God! Amen.

In the beginning was the Word, and the Word was with God,
and the Word was God. (John 1:1)

For You Are the Father's Son

Oftentimes little boys will have an expression on their face or stand with a certain posture that confirms with absolute sureness whose son they are. After imitating my dad, whether consciously or unconsciously, I heard, "Well, you are certainly your father's son."

In every way, Jesus is His Father's Son. He is completely and fully divine. This goes beyond even the way human fathers and sons share DNA. Jesus says, "I and the Father are one" (John 10:30). There is no misunderstanding what Jesus was saying about Himself. The Jews who heard it were so angry they picked up stones to stone Him. They were sure they knew blasphemy when they heard it, and there was no mistaking what Jesus said, except for one detail that they had not considered: He was telling the truth! He and the God the Father are indeed one.

Before Jesus raises Lazarus from the dead, He looks up into heaven and says, "Father, I thank You that You have heard Me. I knew that You always hear Me, but I said this on account of the people standing around, that they may believe that You sent Me" (John 11:41–42). He said these things so that people would know that what He was about to do, His Father would do for Him and also for all who believed in Him. He and the Father are of one mind and one purpose.

John the evangelist writes so succinctly and so eloquently that his words seem worthy of their subject. The Word was there in the beginning, and the Word was with God, and the Word was God. Again, there is no mistaking the clarity and the simplicity of words, but the depth these words plumb is unfathomable. Jesus is, unmistakably, His Father's Son. Amen.

Who has believed what he has heard from us?
And to whom has the arm of the LORD been revealed?
(Isaiah 53:1)

By Your Mighty Power Make Whole

You might be making plans right now to celebrate Christmas and the New Year. You might also be wondering if all your plans will work out. In the past, maybe things did not seem to be coming together like you had expected, and yet at the last minute everything just seemed to click, and it turned out all right.

Isaiah begins the Servant Song (52:13–53:12) with this kind of thought. Who would believe that the Lord would display His great power by sending His Son to suffer? We think that power should be revealed in strength, not in weakness. Throughout the history of Israel, the Lord bore His mighty arm against Israel's enemies on the battlefield. But who would have believed that the Lord would reveal His power in shameful weakness—in the suffering and humiliation of His Son?

In some ways, the tone here may not seem very Christmas-like; it sounds more appropriate for Lent and Holy Week. But we know that the birth of Jesus was the beginning of His humiliation. It was the beginning of His becoming like us so that He could ultimately suffer and die in our place. He had to be like us in every way so that He could take our place under the Law and die for our sins. Many people today still have difficulty with this same idea. They look even at this time of Christmas as a time of being infused with holiday spirit to benefit their neighbors. But the true message of Christmas, the message of the Christian faith, is that God's power is made perfect in the weakness of His Son, born to save all people from their sin. Amen.

But He was wounded for our transgressions;
He was crushed for our iniquities. (Isaiah 53:5)

All Our Ills of Flesh and Soul

Many popular Christian authors and speakers today do not mention sin. It is as if our biggest obstacle in life is that we are not living up to the full potential that God has given us. The message that Isaiah delivers from the Lord is very clear that the obstacles we face in life, whether in our relationships with others or with God Himself, are a result of sin—the sins we commit and the state of the fallen world in which we live.

The "peace on earth and goodwill to men" that we truly desire begins in the humiliation of the Suffering Servant (Isaiah 52:13–53:12). The Servant comes in flesh like ours so that He can stand in our place in every sense. He comes with His perfect flesh to take into Himself our iniquities and sorrows—all of those things we suffer because of the death let loose into this world by the sin of Adam (Romans 5:12–17). He comes to heal all our ills of both flesh and spirit.

Our ills of flesh and soul are not simply our mistakes or imperfections. Our God will not let us think so little of that which is unholy and separates us from Him. To think any less of our sins than what they are is to diminish what He accomplished for us in the birth, life, suffering, death, and resurrection of Jesus, the Lord's Son. And the grandest gift of all is that the Lord delivers to us the benefits of all Jesus has done! All our weaknesses, our depression, all our iniquities are carried away in the body and soul of Him who was born to carry them. We are made perfect in Him. Just as He was high and exalted so shall we be! Amen.

Therefore the Lord Himself will give you a sign. Behold, the virgin shall conceive and bear a son, and shall call His name Immanuel. (Isaiah 7:14)

Here a Maid Was Found with Child

Christians go through a number of trying times—illness, the death of a loved one, family conflict, and others. Sometimes, when problems press in on us from all sides, we lose perspective and wonder whether God is really with us.

King Ahaz of Judah was in a similar bind. Two neighboring kingdoms were pressuring him to join their coalition against Assyria, an aggressor state. But because Ahaz would not join them, they decided to attack, dethrone him, and take his land and people. In the days before their attack, the Lord provided a sign to Ahaz. Through the prophet Isaiah, the Lord said to Ahaz that there will be a virgin who will give birth to a son, and His name will be Immanuel, which means "God is with us."

God is with us in every way. When the Word became flesh and dwelt among us, truly, God was with us. God is not far away in heaven removed from our everyday trials. He knows our trials, for He Himself was hungry and thirsty and knew the ache of loneliness in His own flesh and spirit. He experienced rejection by people who were supposed to be His loving family, even among His own brothers (Matthew 12:46–50). He knows what it is like to be in our place precisely because He was in our place. He continues to be with us, and He promised never to leave or forsake us.

The miracle of Isaiah 7:14 is not just that a virgin will bear a child, though that great miracle came true in the birth of Jesus by Mary, but that Mary's child would bring the abiding and comforting presence of the Lord our God into this world. Amen.

Therefore the Lord Himself will give you a sign. Behold, the virgin shall conceive and bear a son, and shall call His name Immanuel. (Isaiah 7:14)

God Was There
upon His Throne

They go high into the Andes Mountains to visit Machu Picchu in Peru, or they go to Chartres Cathedral in France. They go to famous Buddhist temples in Angkor Wat, Cambodia, and Kyoto, Japan, or to the ancient stone circles in the British Isles like Stonehenge. Some people travel all over the world to visit places where they believe is spiritual energy. They are seeking the "other," the divine, something bigger than themselves, and yet, all the while, many refuse to believe the Christian Gospel that in the womb of a young Palestinian woman was the holiest place of all. There the Creator of the universe came down from heaven and entered into this world in all His holiness and blessedness.

One of the clearest pictures of heaven we have comes from the Book of Isaiah. In a vision, Isaiah beholds the Lord seated on His throne in glory. The six-winged seraphim are flying around, singing, "Holy, holy, holy is the LORD of hosts; the whole earth is full of His glory!" (6:3).

The Good News of Christmas is that Jesus left behind all the splendor of the heavenly throne room and was enthroned in the womb of Mary. People need not travel to the "sacred places" of the earth in order to be closer to God. He chose to come down from heaven and dwell with His people. He continues to be where He has promised: in His Word and in His sacraments of Holy Baptism, the Lord's Supper, and in Holy Absolution. Word, water, bread, and wine—those things may not be very exotic, but they are where the Lord of heavenly splendor has promised Himself to be. There is where we may seek Him. Amen.

In the beginning was the Word, and the Word was with God,
and the Word was God. (John 1:1)

God the Father Was His Source

M any have stood atop the levies along the banks of the mighty Mississippi River and wondered where all the water comes from. North of Minneapolis, Minnesota, the headwaters of the Mississippi River are nothing more than a creek that a boy can jump across. For someone raised much further down the river, this is almost unbelievable. It is difficult to see how mighty that little creek will become before it reaches the sea.

In many ways, Jesus' birth was exactly the opposite. We know that Jesus came down from the greatness of heaven, and when He arrived, He was a baby in swaddling clothes. Sure, the sky was filled with the whole heavenly host the night Jesus was born, but apart from that, Jesus' birth was only as grand as any other birth on earth. It was not until Jesus was transfigured on the mountain that the real holiness of Jesus was clearly shown. Through His ministry, people saw glimpses of that heavenly source in His teaching and miracles (Matthew 7:28; 9:8). They knew they were seeing something greater than what they could see with their eyes. But at Jesus' death on the cross, even His closest disciples had lost all hope that He would be the one to redeem Israel (Luke 24:21).

But when Jesus was resurrected, all the Gospels showed us His glory. Each resurrection appearance seemed to build toward the climax of His glorious ascension into heaven. It was only after Jesus had returned to His source that His majesty and splendor were fully revealed and removed all doubt as to where He came from. He has returned back to the right hand of the Father, still both divine and human to reign for all eternity. Amen.

*In the former time He brought into contempt the land of
Zebulun and the land of Naphtali, but in the latter time He
has made glorious the way of the sea, the land beyond the
Jordan, Galilee of the nations. (Isaiah 9:1)*

The Honor of Galilee
of the Gentiles

Even up through the time of Jesus, Galilee of the Gentiles was considered a poor, lowly place. The girl at Pilate's court could recognize Peter by his Galilean accent probably much the same way in which sophisticated Manhattanites can pick out someone from Brooklyn or the Bronx.

Look at how God had planned to honor poor, humble Galilee. Although it was the first to be conquered and plundered when the Assyrians rolled through, it was also the region where the Savior lived and conducted the majority of His ministry. He was known as Jesus of Nazareth in Galilee. People living in the towns and villages around the lake benefited the most from His teaching and His miracles. The majority of the Twelve were from lowly Galilee, and they came to be not only the disciples of the Lord, but through them the Christian Church grew to be a worldwide movement. Within a century, there were few places in the known world that had not seen a Christian missionary. Not bad for humble Galilee.

God does not leave the spreading of the Gospel to only the rich, the powerful, and the well connected. The humble, ordinary, and everyday Christian—He uses each of us, sinners redeemed by God, to spread the Good News of salvation. After all, evangelism is nothing other than one beggar telling another beggar where to find bread. Amen.

If I say, "Surely the darkness shall cover me, and the light
about me be night," even the darkness is not dark to You;
the night is bright as the day, for darkness is as light with You.
(Psalm 139:11–12)

Even the Darkness
Is Not Dark to You

Military personnel train to conduct operations under the cloak of darkness. Ships can run without lights, pilots can fly and land planes and helicopters, and infantry can maneuver very effectively all while using the technology of night vision goggles. They can continue to operate without disclosing their position to the enemy. These special goggles can work in almost total darkness because they amplify ambient light, effectively turning the night into day where no enemy can hide.

David here says something similar about the Lord. Sometimes in the shame of sin we think God wants nothing to do with us. David knows there is no use trying to skulk in the shadows. He who separated the day from the night and the light from the darkness can easily dispel the darkness simply by speaking into it the light of His Word. There is nowhere to hide in shame from the Lord God.

But there is a certain comfort in this as well. In the words of the psalmist, "Where shall I go from Your Spirit? Or where shall I flee from Your presence? If I ascend to heaven, You are there! If I make my bed in Sheol, You are there! If I take the wings of the morning and dwell in the uttermost parts of the sea, even there Your hand shall lead me, and Your right hand shall hold me" (Psalm 139:7–10). There is no crack we can fall into where the Lord will not be there for us.

Sometimes we are tricked into thinking that who we are and what we do does not really matter to God. But He seeks us out in the shadows of our shame and brings us into His glorious light, restoring us to the honor of His presence. Amen.

*My hand shall be established with him; My arm also shall
strengthen him. The enemy shall not outwit him; the wicked
shall not humble him. I will crush his foes before him and strike
down those who hate him. (Psalm 89:21–23)*

Into Hell His Road
Went Down

After a great victory, a Roman general would be granted a triumph, which usually amounted to a huge parade with the victorious general on a white horse entering Rome accompanied by his victorious legion. When Julius Caesar entered Rome fresh from his campaigns in Gaul, he brought with him the Gallic kings in chains.

After Jesus' death and sometime before His resurrection, Jesus entered hell as a victorious general. He had bested the ancient enemy by making His power perfect in weakness and by His death destroying death itself. Christians must be clear on this. When Jesus went down to hell, He was no longer suffering; He was a conquering hero celebrating the vanquishing of His foe.

But Jesus did suffer hell when He was upon the cross—abandoned by God, alienated from the Father, forsaken. Jesus knew when He left heaven and was to take on human flesh that He would suffer the abandonment of God there on the cross. But having suffered hell for the sins of the whole world on the cross, He suffered in the place of all people so that we would not suffer the estrangement from God in hell. And the descent into hell that He accomplished, He accomplished on behalf of all of us. Jesus entered hell to prove to the devil and his demons that their time was over and their power had been destroyed. At the cross, the old order had passed away and the new had arisen.

Death and hell no longer have power over those who call upon Jesus and are children of God. Jesus was born so that all of this would happen for the sake of God's people. Thanks be to God! Amen.

There was a man sent from God, whose name was John.
He came as a witness, to bear witness about the light,
that all might believe through him. (John 1:6–7)

He Came to Testify
to the Light

He does not play or coach, but the announcer at a baseball game is just as important to the crowd. Among other things, the announcer is there to tell the crowd who is up to bat. Especially in minor league games, the announcer is as much a part of the day's entertainment as the players on the field.

Jesus had an announcer too. His name was John the Baptist. Born six months prior to Jesus, John's birth was also something of a miracle as his mother, Elizabeth, was of advanced years and was thought to be barren. When Mary, pregnant with Jesus, came to visit her cousin Elizabeth, John, still in Elizabeth's womb, leaped for joy in the presence of his Savior. John the Baptist knew by faith, even before he was born, that "the true light, which enlightens everyone, was coming into the world" (John 1:9).

John the evangelist tells us that John the Baptist came as a witness to testify concerning the Light. John the Baptist proclaimed in the wilderness that he was not the Messiah. He proclaimed that the Messiah was coming and all people should prepare for His coming. John's sole mission and purpose in life was finished the day he saw Jesus walking toward him and said, "Behold, the Lamb of God, who takes away the sin of the world!" (John 1:29).

Advent is a time of preparation. It is not just a time to get things ready for the celebration of our Lord's first advent, but also a time to prepare for His second. When Christ comes again, He will come to judge the living and the dead. Advent is a time to prepare our hearts, to repent, and be ready to meet Him who comes with great glory. Amen.

We have seen His glory, glory as of the only Son from the
Father, full of grace and truth. (John 1:14b)

We Beheld His Glory

A favorite pastime during the hot summer afternoons is to head to the movies. Summer blockbusters usually have some superhero triumph over the evil villain and save the planet. After two hours of sitting in the theater, those first few steps outside can really leave us squinting at the gloriously bright summer sun. Depending on how good the movie is, it can feel like the dawning of a new day.

During His earthly ministry, Jesus only once displayed His glory to the disciples and even then it was among a select few. Only Peter, James, and John were there when Moses and Elijah came and spoke with Jesus and He was transfigured on the mountain right before the disciples' eyes. The evangelists record that Jesus' clothes shined like the brightness of the sun. I am sure they had a hard time looking at such a bright light coming from Him.

We do not know exactly what Jesus was talking about with Moses and Elijah, but we do know what Jesus did once He came down from the mountain. He and His disciples stepped out of the bright glory of Jesus' divinity, and Jesus announced He was headed to Jerusalem where He would be betrayed into the hands of sinful men, be crucified, and on the third day be raised from the dead (Mark 10:32).

We know that Jesus was born to be vastly superior to any superhero devised by Hollywood. He truly conquered evil and saved the planet from the ravages of not only a cruel and oppressive evil genius, Satan, but in His death, He destroyed the very power of death itself. It is no wonder that the shepherds seeing and hearing the angelic host herald the birth of the world's savior were fixated on the glorious message. They walked out of their darkness and stumbled blinking to see the babe born in Bethlehem. Amen.

*He will receive blessing from the LORD and righteousness from
the God of his salvation. (Psalm 24:5)*

Who May Ascend
the Hill of the Lord?

There are a number of peaks on the easternmost range in Colorado that are above a breathtaking 14,000 feet. Many of them require no technical climbing at all and are just rugged mountain treks that lead to some amazing views. Regardless of the difficulty of the mountain, some preparation is in order. A climber must bring along enough food and water to last the day's climb, along with extra in case of an emergency.

David knows that to climb the holy hill of Mount Zion a similar thought to preparation is in order. This is God's holy mountain. Just as the Lord had declared Sinai to be His holy mountain and would not allow any of the unconsecrated Israelites on the mountain (Exodus 19:10–15), David knows that to go up to the Lord on Zion, one must be prepared to meet Him. Only he may ascend "who has clean hands and a pure heart, who does not lift up his soul to what is false and does not swear deceitfully" (Psalm 24:4).

Almost always in the Divine Service, preceding the Service of the Word is a Service of Preparation that includes the Confession and Absolution of sin. We know that as we approach the Lord in His holy house and hear His Holy Word, and eat at His Holy Supper, we should prepare to enter into His presence by confessing our sin and receiving the blessed assurance of His Word: "I forgive you all your sins."

Advent, too, is about that kind of preparation. Getting ready to celebrate the festival of the Lord's nativity, yes, but even more so, preparing for His triumphant return. Why should we be preparing for the Lord's return? Because He is coming to judge the living and the dead. Prepare the way of the Lord. Get ready. He is coming soon! Amen.

*He had no form or majesty that we should look at Him, and no
beauty that we should desire Him. He was despised and rejected
by men; a man of sorrows, and acquainted with grief; and as
one from whom men hide their faces He was despised, and we
esteemed Him not. (Isaiah 53:2b–3)*

His Heroic Course Began

The Superman franchise has certainly made an impact over the last several decades. Originally a comic book superhero, he easily made the transition into television and even feature films. Most people are familiar with Superman's two identities: Superman and Clark Kent, mild-mannered reporter. It is a feature of the franchise that Clark's true identity as Superman is hidden.

When the divine Word took upon Himself human flesh and became Jesus, He chose to hide His divine identity. When He would encounter demons, He would silence them so that they would not reveal His true identity until it was the right time. Even when on the cross, people mocking Jesus were tempting Him to reveal His true self: " 'If you are the Son of God, come down from the cross.' So also the chief priests, with the scribes and elders, mocked Him, saying, 'He saved others; He cannot save Himself. He is the King of Israel; let Him come down now from the cross, and we will believe in Him' " (Matthew 27:40b–42).

Jesus' entire heroic mission relied on the humility of who He was and the humiliation He was willing to endure in order to save all people from their sins. It was a completely undercover operation—the tactics of which the old enemy never suspected. Jesus took away the guilt of sin by bearing in His own human flesh the guilt of our sin. The perfect obedience required by God under the Law, He completed on behalf of all people. He did not look like much in His mild-mannered disguise, but when He came into His glory at the cross, the whole earth was saved. Amen.

*His appearance was so marred, beyond human semblance, and
His form beyond that of the children of mankind.
(Isaiah 52:14b)*

A Face Easily Dismissed

Our nation's intelligence agencies attempt to recruit some of the best and brightest young people in our nation. One thing is always a requirement for the application: a photograph. They want a certain look—attractive, but not too attractive, slim and athletic but not strikingly so. They are looking for a nondescript ability to blend in. Spies should never draw too much attention to themselves by their physical appearance or mannerisms.

The Suffering Servant in Isaiah 52:13–53:12 is a little more than that. He is so physically marred that He is perhaps even unworthy to be a priest. Sons of Aaron were forbidden from serving as priests if in their body they possessed any physical blemish or deformity (Leviticus 21:17–23). The Suffering Servant certainly was not noteworthy in His appearance at all. It would be as easy to overlook and discount Him just as the majority of us overlook the countless homeless on the streets of our cities. Our world is obsessed with physical appearance. And those who are deemed not beautiful enough are excluded from having any importance.

But Jesus used His physical appearance to His definite advantage. When He finally appeared before Pontius Pilate, he could hardly believe this poor Galilean prophet and healer was guilty of the crimes charged against Him by the religious rulers (John 18:33). What Pilate meant as incredulity, Jesus and the Father had planned before all time. There is no one that Jesus came to save that does not matter or who could be easily overlooked. Those who are invisible or ugly as our world defines them are redefined in Christ. If Jesus took upon Himself all our ugliness, then it was so that we might receive the beauty endowed on Him by the Father. Amen.

And the Word became flesh and dwelt among us,
and we have seen His glory, glory as of the only Son from
the Father, full of grace and truth. (John 1:14)

Who Is He?

Maybe you have seen the film too many times, but for the first-time viewer of *The Wizard of Oz,* there is a tremendous anti-climax in the throne room of the great and powerful Oz. Ever since Dorothy woke up in the land of Oz with Munchkins staring at her, she has been on this journey to Oz to see the great wizard who can hopefully help her return to Kansas. It turns out that the great and powerful Oz is a little swarthy man behind a curtain pulling levers and speaking into a microphone to magnify his voice to make himself appear far greater than he really is. It is a huge letdown.

The film mirrored some of the sentiments increasingly being preached in mainline churches in that day and into ours. "Pay no attention to the man behind the curtain. . . . Those miracles recorded in the Gospels are merely narrative constructs from the more developed Christian Church in a later period seeking to make Jesus into something more than He originally claimed to be." If that is our understanding, much of the New Testament is certainly not much more than the fearsome pronouncements of the great and powerful Oz.

Even more insidious is the idea that Dorothy and her friends had it in them the whole time to provide their own rescue—Dorothy to return home, the Scarecrow to have a brain, the Tin Man to have a heart, and the Lion to have courage. "Salvation comes from within" is certainly a popular message among folks who would ignore God's gift in Christ.

How refreshing it is, then, to hear these words from the Gospel: "We have seen His glory, glory as of the only Son from the Father, full of grace and truth." Amen.

But He was wounded for our transgressions; He was crushed for our iniquities; upon Him was the chastisement that brought us peace, and with His stripes we are healed. (Isaiah 53:5)

He Gives What We Need to Live

Many folks feel uneasy about becoming an organ donor. While organ donation can bring a new lease on life to the person who receives the organ, it almost invariably comes as a result of another's death. Some of the commonly donated organs are hearts, livers, kidneys, and corneas.

When the eternal Word decided to take on human flesh and be born into this world, He knew that it would result not just in His suffering but in His death. In offering up His heart to us, He gives us the ability to love both God and neighbor. By giving us His liver and kidneys, He provided a means to cleanse us from all impurities and the toxins of sin, the world and our own flesh. By giving us His corneas, He gave us the ability to see all the more clearly and focus not only on everything that our God has given us through His Son, but on all that our heavenly Father has set before us.

This is obviously a metaphor of what Jesus truly gave us in giving us Himself. We know that He offered up not only His organs to all of humanity but also His whole life so that we might have the life our Father in heaven truly intended for us to have. As children of God, we know God created us for a purpose. He willingly gave Himself in this way so that He might be a true substitute for us. Jesus did not just suffer in the flesh with us, but completely *for us.* In sending His Son, God the Father has provided for us a new lease on life with Him forever! Amen.

*Who shall ascend the hill of the L*ORD*?*
And who shall stand in His holy place? He who has clean
hands and a pure heart, who does not lift up His soul to what
is false and does not swear deceitfully. (Psalm 24:3–4)

Who Shall Ascend
the Hill of the Lord?

Wash your hands for supper!" was a familiar command in my house. My mom knew that all of us boys needed to have our hands washed. There was no telling what we had been up to either down at the creek trying to catch minnows and crayfish or out in the woods digging for bugs. It was a matter of fact that you did not come to the table with dirty hands. Period.

At the Divine Service, of course, one of the first things we do is wash our hands, metaphorically anyway. We confess to God our sins, and we receive the forgiveness won for us by Christ at the cross. Then it is right that we come to hear His Word and eat at His Supper prepared for us.

When I was a kid, I hated to wash my hands. I could never see any dirt worth washing off to begin with. I thought it was a waste of time. But my mom knew, as probably most moms know, that I definitely needed to wash my hands before coming to the table. We often treat confession and absolution with the same childish contempt—I mean, at least I have not killed anybody, right? "But I say to you that everyone who is angry with his brother will be liable to judgment" (Matthew 5:22a). Uh oh. I have.

Confession can be a real downer. We like to think we are not all that bad. But confession affords us the opportunity to say the same thing about our sins that our Lord says about our sins. Our Lord certainly intends His word of absolution as a gift and as a way to show us that in that one word of forgiveness, He has washed our hands and cleansed our hearts to be worthy to be in His presence. Amen.

The people who walked in darkness have seen a great light;
those who dwelt in a land of deep darkness, on them has light
shined. (Isaiah 9:2)

The People Have Seen
a Great Light

There is a commonly accepted pattern in working with those who suffer from addictions that they cannot accept help unless there is no other option, unless they have reached "rock bottom."

Judah had reached rock bottom. The desolation wrought by the king of Assyria was total. All the fields, vineyards, flocks, and houses were destroyed. The only folks left were the poorest of the poor and the least significant of people. Anyone who could work toward rebuilding anything in the region was carried off into exile in Babylon. The only food left in the whole area was some dairy from small flocks (curds) and wild honey (Isaiah 7:15) but out of this insignificant remnant would come the Savior of the people, God's Servant.

God had promised that the dark gloom cast over the whole land would not be eternal. He would not let His people suffer in exile and struggle in subsistence living forever. After they finally experienced the just results of having abandoned the Lord and His ways, He would provide a rescue and a source of blessing for His people, a true and proper King to rule His people forever. "For to us a child is born, to us a son is given; and the government shall be upon His shoulder, and His name shall be called Wonderful Counselor, Mighty God, Everlasting Father, Prince of Peace" (Isaiah 9:6).

In providing this new Prince of Peace, the Lord was providing for Israel the kind of king that their former kings had been only in name. He would be a king like David but even greater than David. He would reign with righteousness and justice forever.

We who look to God in all things, even in the midst of great suffering from the bottom of our pit, know that God does not permit a humiliation for where He has not planned an even greater exaltation! Amen.